HowExpert Pre

I0016668

How To Podcast

Your Step By Step Guide To Podcasting

HowExpert

For more tips related to this topic, visit HowExpert.com/podcast.

Recommended Resources

- HowExpert.com – Quick 'How To' Guides on All Topics from A to Z by Everyday Experts.
- HowExpert.com/free – Free HowExpert Email Newsletter.
- HowExpert.com/books – HowExpert Books
- HowExpert.com/courses – HowExpert Courses
- HowExpert.com/clothing – HowExpert Clothing
- HowExpert.com/membership – HowExpert Membership Site
- HowExpert.com/affiliates – HowExpert Affiliate Program
- HowExpert.com/writers – Write About Your #1 Passion/Knowledge/Expertise & Become a HowExpert Author.
- HowExpert.com/resources – Additional HowExpert Recommended Resources
- YouTube.com/HowExpert – Subscribe to HowExpert YouTube.
- Instagram.com/HowExpert – Follow HowExpert on Instagram.
- Facebook.com/HowExpert – Follow HowExpert on Facebook.

3

Table of Contents

Recommended Resources............................2

Introduction 8

Podcasting History 9

What You're Getting in this Book...................... 11

Chapter 1: How to get Started................... 13

Developing the Idea of Your Podcast.................13

Who's Hosting? 15

Is Your Content Free-Flowing, or Written Down?
....16

How Long is Each Episode?................................17

Conclusion 17

Chapter 2: Producing Your Show.............. 19

Researching and Purchasing Your Equipment ..19

Where Do You Record? 22

The Recording Methods 25

Audio Editing 27

Theme Music *29*

Exporting Your MP3 File........................ 31

ID3 Tags and Why They Matter: *31*

Chapter 3: Setting Up Your Website.........34

Choosing a Webhost, and Setting Up Wordpress

.... *34*

Wordpress Themes.............................. *39*

When Should You Start Publishing Episodes?...40

Logos/Album Covers............................. *40*

Submitting Your Podcast to Directories. 41

Take Feedburner Feed and Place It Into iTunes

.... 44

Chapter 4: Podcast Promotions 46

How to Market Your Podcast *46*

Search Engines................................ *47*

Marketing Via Other Podcasts........................*51*

Traditional Ads *53*

Traditional Media *55*

Other Marketing Mediums *57*

Chapter 5: Social Media for Podcasts **59**

Facebook *59*

Twitter *62*

Using Both Facebook and Twitter Effectively

.... *63*

Chapter 6: Monetizing Your Podcast **65**

Advertising *65*

Affiliate Sales *66*

Direct Sales *67*

Offering a Service *68*

Merchandising *69*

Premium Podcasting *70*

Using Monetization Effectively *70*

Chapter 7: Creating Your Community **73**

How to Create That Community? *74*

Remember: Community Takes Time *76*

Conclusion **77**

Appendix A: List of Links 78

Resources about Podcasting 78

Books 78

Podcasts.....................................78

Audio Editing Tutorials 79

Podcast Equipment Sources............................... 79

Software.....................................79

Hardware.................................... 80

List of SEO guides 80

Appendix B: How to Do Basic Edits in Garageband and Audacity 81

Audacity 81

The Basics of Audacity Editing 82

Garage Band 85

How to Edit and Record Audio on Garageband 85

Recommended Resources......................... 89

Introduction

Broadcasting oneself over the airwaves and internet has become a lot easier over the last 10 years. Companies and individuals can now present their viewpoints and products through any number of communication methods. These include email, blogging, advertising, and so much more. But how can anyone create great content that reaches thousands, and maybe even millions? One of the best methods that has developed in the last 6 years for expressing and sharing content is podcasting.

Podcasting is by definition a recorded audio broadcast that is designed to be played whenever, and with whatever the user likes. This technology phenomenon is currently crossing the world, with thousands of companies and individuals having the opportunity to create unique and popular content. What's great about this medium is that pretty much anyone can create content as long as they have a microphone, a computer, and an internet connection. And this freedom has so much potential.

Podcasting is a great medium for both hobbyist podcasters and companies to use to create material. Hobbyists can use it to express and explore their own interests, as well as meet people, gain experience, and just have fun. Meanwhile businesses can use the medium to create content, give themselves a voice for their audience, and even allow potential customers to "sample" their content in order to see if they enjoy it.

But that is only the beginning for podcast's potential. Radio shows are able to spread their content past the original broadcasting date. Non-profits and organizations can give quick updates on their projects and items. The possibilities are endless. However, the experience and professionalism behind a lot of podcasts scares many into saying no to trying to create similar content, since they feel like they are not up to the industry standard. However, podcasting is a lot easier than you could ever think. There are award-winning podcasts that are done with the simplest possible set-up, and are enjoyed by thousands of people. Besides, if people are interested in the content, then they will listen, whether or not your content was recorded in a professional studio, or your basement. But before we get into the method of podcast, let's explore the history of the podcast.

Podcasting History

Like all technological marvels, podcasting is built upon a foundation of technological steps that developed over many years. The first development necessary for podcasting was the Internet. The internet was originally invented in the late 70s/early 80s by a number of universities who wanted to make it easy to transfer information between them. However, the most important development for podcasting was the creation of Internet Transmission control Protocol. This technical development allowed audio to be transferred over the internet. The next notable development in computing technologies was the serial port microphone, which allowed audio to be recorded on a computer easily. This recording technique also required a universal file style, which allowed the creators to make the MP3, which is the universal standard for audio files. Website developments allowed for the creation of the weblog, or blog, as we currently know it. When companies developed blogging software, they also created Really Simple Syndication, or RSS feeds, which allow for updates to be streamed out to the numerous websites.

While the idea of releasing online radio shows or doing audio blogging was not a new idea, the concept of podcasts made this idea mainstream. The "Podcasting revolution" was originally started by MTV VJ Adam Curry in 2004. Curry stirred the pot by broadcasting his own recorded online radio show called *The Daily Source Code*. Future podcast celebrities like Tech-TV creator Leo Laporte and wannabe radio DJ Brian Ibbot were inspired by Curry's technological move, so they each began their own podcasts as well. Laporte would go on to start one of the greatest podcast networks ever made, TWIT.TV, while Ibbot would host his show, Coverville, for over 7 years, and record over 800 episodes. Moreover, all of this activity was at a point where the term "podcast" hadn't even been developed.

The term was introduced in a column written by Ben Hammersly of the *UK Guardian*. He wrote a report on this movement of online radio shows, and was offering up a list of terms that could describe this movement. Podcast was simply the one that stuck around. The podcasting movement was reported on by a number of newspapers, magazines, and tech sources. This attracted a lot of people to the medium, who began listening. They found the content to be fantastic. Many of these first listeners went on to create their own shows, and market them to others. The movement took fire on the internet very quickly.

At first, podcasts were released via a normal RSS podcast feed. Each episode had to be downloaded individually by the users. So, some programmers teamed up to create RSS clients that were able to read the uniqueness of these files, and download the files directly to your ITunes library. However, the big change happened when iTunes developed a new directory for podcasters to insert their podcast feeds into. This directory also made it easy for people to subscribe and download. Now you just have to click subscribe on the iTunes directory, and the episode downloads directly to your account, ready for you to listen to. There are some other developments that have occurred over the years, but the most important development is the ability to collect these feeds, and download the shows quickly.

What You're Getting in this Book

If you've downloaded this book, then it's likely that you have a strong interest in either how podcasting works, or in starting your show. It's probably both. So, this book's sole purpose is to provide you with the basics for setting up your podcast, recording it, sharing, promoting it, and using it to the fullest extent. This process will take time and effort, but the product you will produce in the end will be well on its way to doing something altogether excellent.

Chapter 1 is specifically focused on your podcast's niche. It will help you make the right choices about what your show is about, and how you are going to produce it.

Chapter 2 explores the technical angles, including choosing hardware, software, choosing your set-up, and learning how to record and create a product that can be placed on iTunes.

Chapter 3 talks more about your website, how to set it up specifically for podcasting, and how to get your podcast into iTunes, the world's largest Podcast directories.

Chapter 4 is the promotion chapter. We will cover all of the important details related to your show, and how to get your name out actively.

Chapter 5 is especially focused on creating an effective social media profile across the many social networks, including Facebook, Twitter, and much more.

Chapter 6 covers a subject that many would love; monetizing your show. Here is where you will explore the details of how to make a profit off of your show, and whether trying to do so is even worth your time.

Chapter 7 is dedicated to doing one of the most important things for your podcast; attempting to create community around you and your show.

Hopefully, all of these concepts will give you a deeper look at how to make an altogether excellent product for you, your company, and your future listeners.

Chapter 1: How to get Started

Developing the Idea of Your Podcast

You're here, and you're ready to podcast. I bet you want to just jump in and start. The first thing you need to consider before even buying equipment is, what's your podcast going to be about? There are a lot of people who want to do a podcast but don't have a particular focus or idea. But who wouldn't want to be a radio host, and talk away, and be known for their opinion? This is an appealing vision, but this perspective has a tendency to create sub-par shows without a great point, which are just a set of banter that isn't terribly enjoyable to listen to. So, when starting down the path to podcasting, there are a number of things that will be worth considering.

The best idea for a new podcast is to start out with a center. This center is the key to the whole picture. And the center for almost all podcasts is the audience. The audience is made up of all the people that you want to attract to your show. They are the ones that will surround you and fuel you. So, consider what they want. Often, people are looking for unique products that focus on a single niche. They aren't looking for a new general tech show, or another movie review show that touches every single film in the theatres. There needs to be something unique to your podcast that no one else can fill. Here are some ideas for finding that special something.

- **Consider Your Interests**: Everyone has subjects or hobbies that they enjoy. And it's likely that there are others who love the subject just as much as you do. So, what are your loves? Is it books? If so, then do a book review, or book-club show. Are you a mean golfer? Then talk about either golf on television, or the latest developments, or even your own tips for the new golfer.

- **Acknowledge Your expertise:** Another consideration to take when choosing a show is to ask yourself what are you an expert in? By having expertise in something, then you would have the opportunity to express that expertise to a larger audience, and to further your own expertise by researching deeper into your subject. Some of the best shows are based around niche experts, who express their interest passionately through the airwaves.

Now, make sure that you separate expertise from opinion. All of us are opinionated about something. But if you can mix that opinion with either a unique angle, or "bent" as some call it, this angle brings new light to your opinion, and makes it valuable. However, your opinion shouldn't be just it. Otherwise, you are just another clanging gong who wants to be noticed. Your expertise should give value to your audience, and make them consider things that otherwise might be forgotten.

- **See What Others are Doing, and Do What They're Not:** This is always a great way to find a unique niche. Here's a good example: There are a lot of homeschool podcasts out there hosted by homeschool parents. But what about a homeschool podcast hosted by a homeschool graduate? That's what originally inspired the podcast Confessions of a Homeschool Graduate (CHGradio.org).

It's the basic idea of what Wired Editor Chris Anderson called "The Long Tail." To explain this idea, I need you to imagine a long tail, which represents the market for your product, and where the process is determined by demand and desire. To explain this, I will use the classic example of tech podcasts. At the top are shows like *This Week in Tech* and *Tekzilla*. These shows are basic tech shows that touch on just a little bit of everything. There are a lot of general tech shows out there, competing to be number one. But none of them can beat the original *This Week in Tech*. As you search further, you can find smaller niche shows, like *The Mac-cast,* or *Maximum PC.* There are fewer shows in these categories, but it's still fairly wide. If you continue further down the "Tail," you'll find unique shows dedicated to PC gaming, or to Mac accessories. Eventually, you get down to shows that are dedicated to just one computer type, or how to do one specific thing. This kind of focus is great for businesses, and for podcasts. So, it's worth looking into what has been done already. By choosing something that hasn't been done, then you won't have any competition, and will have impact longer.

But if you choose the path of a very small niche, you need to ask yourself "Is there enough content?" One mistake that podcasters could make is choosing a subject that doesn't have enough content to support its model. *Podcasting for Dummies* author Tee Morris' best example for this was "a show centered around the intricacies of reattaching lost buttons onto lady's blouses." Obviously, this idea is very limited, and probably could only last 1 to 3 episodes. Yet this is certainly a great concept for a segment, or a small part of a larger show. So, consider your niches carefully. But whatever niche you choose, take advantage of it, and use it effectively.

Who's Hosting?

This may seem like a silly question. But it is still one that we should engage. Who's hosting the show? The obvious answer is yourself. But is there anyone else? Many shows can be done with only one person. *The Quick and Dirty Tips* network uses the solo method to emphasize the expertise of their host. Also, the goal of each episode is to inform you. But what if more than one opinion is required for your product? This is where multiple hosts come in. The natural conversation between experts makes listening to the opinions of others a lot more interesting. Hearing one man express his opinion sounds like a lecture. The banter and conversation that comes with multiple hosts can make a show infinitely more entertaining. It also is easier to produce, since conversation flows more naturally than the lecture. It's also pleasant to listen to.

Other methods that podcasters need to consider are the panel-style and the interview. Panels require a number of voices, which are either collected in one place or call in over the internet and are recorded. Panels are great, since they bring in a number of experts, who focus their perspectives on specific subjects. These panels can be weekly conversations about something unique, or a one-time gathering of experts. This kind of podcast requires a lot more microphones and/or computers. But it is a great way to explore subjects in depth.

Interviews are something that all of us would love to do. Having the chance to talk to experts about their subject, learn what we can, and share that conversation with the world. This method requires being able to connect up with expert, being able to record them on the fly, and keep things simple.

Is Your Content Free-Flowing, or Written Down?

Most podcasts are based on the conversational abilities of the host(s). If they know their subject, then all they need to create more content is their memory, and some notes. However, some podcasts can just be a man reading a script.

The classic example of this is the podcast *Escape Pod*. Each episode is simply a short story read aloud by either the host, or a voice actor. What makes this content great is that you can produce it by simply reading a story, and releasing. It won't require any segments, or single thoughts. Of course, you will have to have the script ready. But as long as it's ready, then you will be ready as well.

How Long is Each Episode?

Podcasts come in many lengths, from a 2 minute speech, to a 2 hour long ramble. We all know that most shows will have shorter episodes, and longer episodes. But we need to choose our goals for each episode. The length of the episode often relies on the content.

So, let's say you want to make a really short show. How do you do that? A great model to follow for this type of show is *Merriam-Webster's Word of the Day*. Their show is a short summary of information about a word. Its shortness makes it fun to listen to quickly, and apply to your life. It also gives you the content up front. No fuss or muss.

On the other side are shows like *This Week in Tech,* or *TWIT* for short. This show is news-based, and has to cover this news in a limited time period. Often, the news stories are based around things that are centered in the opinion of others. So, having the opportunity to express these opinions will take time. And that's where the hour-long shows come from. Also, shows that are based around the method used by talk show hosts also need that time to express multiple opinions, and explore the many angles to the story.

Conclusion

Now you have an idea of the content you want created. You know what your goals for each episode are, how long you want them to be, and even whether you want a co-host. You should know what you want, and your goals.

But how should you progress forward? The easiest way is to make a plan for the future. Come up with future goals, and plans. Also, figure out how often you want to release content, and how much effort you want to put in each episode. Don't worry about how long it takes up front. The first episode is always the hardest. As you get used to creating episodes on a repetitive basis, you will also find it easier to create the episodes, and enjoy it more.

But now that you've planned all of this out, it's time to figure out how to do it.

Chapter 2: Producing Your Show

Researching and Purchasing Your Equipment

Now, you have an idea for what you want to do with your show. It's time to start equipping yourself with recording equipment. Podcasting can cost as much, or as little as you like it to. But what is required for recording a podcast?

Microphone of some kind (either a professional microphone, or a headset microphone. Even a laptop microphone could be used.)

- Computer (you obviously have that, since you are reading this eBook)
- Audio recording software, like Audacity, Garageband, or Adobe Audition

These tools are the absolute essential for a podcaster. However you should also consider investing in the following tools sometime in your podcasting future.

- Pop screen (a simple device that keeps you from creating audio spikes every time you pronounce a T, P, or B)
- Portable recorder
- A livestreaming website like Ustream.tv or Justin.tv
- Noise Gate
- Skype Account

As a podcaster, you can pay as much or as little as you like for podcasting equipment. You can buy just a headset and use Audacity, a free program, to record your podcast. You can also go the other direction and invest heavily in radio-standard equipment. Just remember that whatever way you invest, the equipment doesn't make the best show. However, having better equipment will last you a longer period, and serve you better in the long-term.

Before really getting into the recording process, one should look at the potential equipment. Some podcasters use the microphone installed in their laptop, but that isn't the best place to start podcasting with. The problem with it is that the microphone picks up all the sounds in the room. So, even if you shift in your chair, the microphone will pick it up. This is not good for any recording, and is terribly distracting for the listener.

The first place to look if you want to buy equipment on a cheap basis is your local tech store. There, you can pick up a cheap gaming headset with a microphone. The set-up for that microphone will let you focus your microphone's sound range, and keep it from picking up background sounds.

If the podcaster wants to take a step up in equipment, they should look into podcasting kits. Some of the best places include Musiciansfriend.com and Amazon. These two places offer microphones and mixers as well as recording kits for users of home studios. But the most notable kit is the Behringer Podcastudio. This kit can be from 100 to 200 dollars in cost. There are two different versions. The first has a USB connection, while the second has a Firewire connection. Both come with a mic, a stand, a sound board, and the simplest software. They are good kits to begin with at reasonable cost.

Of course, if you have the money, you can purchase much higher-priced equipment sets. These sets usually contain a special microphone that won't have problems with sound. It will be connected to a crane-like contraption that keeps it from being bumped. The equipment also comes with a large mixer (great for more than one microphone), wires for input, output, and recording. Often, these set-ups do well with more than one computer. This kind of equipment does make your room look like a radio studio. But the quality that comes out of this equipment is amazing. Your podcast will sound almost like an episode from NPR.

As you're investigating your equipment for podcasting, it's also worth considering what kind of audio software you choose. The first software to consider is Audacity (audacity.sourceforge.com). This software is used by audio engineers and podcasters alike. It's a universal editor used by all computers. Audacity provides great starting software that will edit your audio, and make it sound fantastic. However, the software is open source, which means that it can be glitchy at times, and not have all of the best tools for audio editing.

The next software that is often used is Garage Band. A mac-centric software that is normally installed on new Macs, it's another great source for audio editing. This software contains a number of sound loops, editing features, and even a file type that is specifically focused on podcasting. It's a great piece of software for podcasters. It does require practice, but once you've mastered it, you will find an excellent product.

Now, there are professional software packages for the podcast producer, like Adobe Audition, and Apple Logic studio. This software often costs hundreds of dollars, but gives you the best quality, and the best tools. But no matter what you do, and whether you invest hundreds of dollars in your software or nothing at all, the audio editing process is the same.

The next investment to consider as you go forward is the investment of time. How much time do you have to invest in the production of the show? This doesn't involve just the production of the audio, but also maintaining a website and social presence. So, how much time can you commit? Give yourself an estimate of what you can do, and what needs to be done. Then, plan around it. But make sure that in everything you do, you're doing because you love it, not because of a sense of duty.

Where Do You Record?

All of us have offices or other places where we do our work. Similarly, there is likely somewhere where you will constantly record. It could be an office, a den, an attic, maybe even a closet. Where you choose to record will affect the quality of recording that you will have. Here are some tips that should help you find the best place to record:

- **Look for Somewhere That is Undisturbed**: Places that are high traffic in your home will be a bad choice. Make sure that when you sit down to record, you don't have to worry about disturbances and distractions.

- **Keep That Area Clean:** One of the things about technology is that wires and items get easily mixed up, and are hard to manage overall. This twisted up wires and gadgets make it hard to keep equipment in good condition. Also, having a cluttered desk means that if you move, it's likely that your microphone will pick up your sound.

- **Consider Putting Your Equipment Away:** One of the side effects of leaving equipment out is that kids, cats, dogs, and clumsy roommates may break something that you need. So, make sure to take good care of your equipment, and consider who else uses your space.

- **Listen to the Jungle:** Your recording spot may have a lot of noise in it that you wouldn't hear. But the microphone will. So, consider things like air conditioners, computer fans, passing trains, and everything. A great way to test how much "feedback" is in

22

your area is to turn on your microphone, and just record the background. That will give you a basic feeling for what could be recorded.

- **Change Scenery If There's a Problem:** If your choice of recording place is full of sound, then it will be worth considering moving. Choose somewhere with far less sound. That way, you won't have too many problems.

All of these little changes will help you make the best possible recording, so that as many people as possible can enjoy it.

Other Things to Consider: There are always tools that we forget to count. These include online accessible web tools for organization as well as small accessories for your microphone, your website, and your performance. So, here's a more detailed exploration of these tools:

- **Pop Filter:** This small accessory is important for high quality podcast recordings. It acts as a gate for the sound. Any and all speaking goes through it, but the cloth placed between you and the microphone keeps it from picking up the distinct sounds of the T, and the P. These sounds release small bursts of air from your mouth, which the microphone picks up. These sounds are extremely distracting, and are a nuisance for the listener. By buying a pop filter, or making your own version of the device, you can remove the sound problem from your production values.

- **Skype Account:** Podcasting often involves contacting people from all over the world. One of the best ways to do this is using Skype. You can call other Skypers, access other phone numbers, and even use it to record phone calls. This service is free, but for accessories like calling others, you will have to pay extra. Also, to record a Skype phone call, there are a number of pieces of software that allow you to do this for a fairly cheap price. You can also use a physical setup, with a portable recorder to record calls in a higher quality. But it all depends on your individual choice.

- **Portable Recorder:** Some podcast recording set-ups may benefit from the use of portable recorders. It makes public recording sessions work out very well. The Zoom series of recorders is preferred by most podcasters because of the ease of use, and the quality audio.

- **Noise Gate:** This device acts as a filter for your sound. As you record your podcast, you can stream your sound through this Noise Gate, and the Noise Gate will remove the sounds in the room, as well as balancing both the low and high points. It makes the editing process easier, and it also brings the show into a higher-quality setting.

- **Google Accounts:** This is a collection of tools. If you haven't seen, Google has created a number of tools for everyone to use in everyday life. This includes things like Gmail (email account and a great tool for contacting), Google Docs (online word processor), Google Call (online scheduling tool), Google Adsense (opportunity to put ads on website, and make money), and even Google reader (RSS feed reader, great for checking blogs). These are all great tools for scheduling, notes, and whatever else a podcaster may need. The online nature also makes it great for sharing information and ideas with co-hosts. The best thing about all of these tools: they're free!!

- **Ustream.TV** One of the prospects of a good podcast is the opportunity to record their show in front of a live audience. Services like Ustream.tv offer podcasters the chance to do this for free, with only the occasional ad breaking up transmissions. You can also record your stream, and play it back later for those who are interested. There are upgraded versions which allow for multi-cam set ups, and even ad-free playing. But it matters on the podcast. There are other services that actively record the stream if you desire, including Talkshoe Radio, and Justin.TV. However, Ustream.tv is the most recommended service.

Do the Tools Make the Podcaster? One of the things you need to ask as a podcaster is whether you define the equipment, or if the equipment defines you. A great podcast can have some of the most basic equipment, but still make great content. A horrible podcast can have great sound, but say nothing new to the world. This kind of community is unhelpful, and not good to focus on. So, don't focus on what you have, or don't have. Focus on making content that people want to hear.

However, don't be afraid of working to upgrade, and make the best sound in your budget. The more that you invest, the longer your equipment will last. Consider what the long-term value will be.

The Recording Methods

By now, you should know what kind of show you're doing. You know whether you need a co-host, and whether it will last an hour or 5 minutes.

So, how do you record an episode? The process is more difficult than you think. First, consider whether you want to have a show that's edited together, or is a one-take wonder. The two particular methods are unique in their own rights, and have pros and cons to them that are worth consideration.

- **One-Take Wonder**: This is where you, the host, simply tap the record button, and talks away. This is the normal method for multi-host podcasts. The conversations are usually recorded in their fullest extent. These recordings don't often need a lot of editing. Some basic edits should be done, in order to add theme music, or transitions. But overall, this method is simple.

Pros:

-Simplicity of recording

-Natural conversation

-easy to produce and release

Cons:

-Mistakes are likely to stay in

-May not be the best choice for solo-casts

-Less professional sound

- **Multi-Takes:** This process allows you to record multiple segments into your show. You would record the different parts of the podcasts at different times, and edit them together with transitions, sound effects, and even theme music. This method does take a lot of time, and can be stressful.

Pros:

-Professional sound

-Great transitions

-Potentially longer shows

-opportunity to fix mistakes

-opportunity to gain experience in audio editing

Cons:

-More work

-Having to mix multiple elements into it

-large time requirement

Both methods have inherent value; make the decision based on your show, and what you wish to produce with your time.

Audio Editing

Whether you use Audacity or Garage Band, you will have a lot of editing to do. You will want to work to edit the audio so that it sounds as professional as possible. Now, some podcasts need more editing than others. I've found that recordings of a single person need far more edits, since the language isn't as natural. If someone flubs up in a conversation, then it isn't as much of a distraction.

So, as you re-listen to your recording, watch out for certain things.

- Mic Pops (Slight bumps, or bursts of unaltered sound. Very distracting, and not fun to hear)
- Background noise (listeners do not want to hear your cat hacking a hairball in the back of your explanation of the stock market)
- Points where the sound or music is too soft, or too loud (You want to talk over your music, yet let it be heard by all)
- Abrupt edits (This includes edits of sound that make your talking sound forced)
- Weird noises (Any sound that shouldn't be there)

When you find these sounds, don't be afraid of edits. These edits will make you sound more refined. It also helps listeners ignore your flubs in speech.

Now, audio editors use audio effects in order to cause certain changes. They are often easy to use, and only need a quick highlight of an audio sample, then the access to the software. Here are some effects for users that will improve your editing ability:

- **Amplify:** This simple tool allows you to lift or lower volume levels for a select point in time.

- **Fade-In/Out:** This tool is great for podcast openings, transitions, or endings. It tells the audio to increase from 0 volume to the chosen time, or to lower until the volume reaches 0.

- **Repeat:** This effect is useful when you have a musical loop or sound effect that you need to play again.

- **Chris's Dynamic Compressor:** An effect very specific to Audacity, this was discovered by Daniel Lewis of *The Audacity to Podcast*. This effect is useful for recordings, since the software is able to balance out all points where the sound is too low, or too high. This effect does require extra work to install, but the effect it will have on your podcast is mind-blowing. You can find the file for the effect at this link, thanks to Daniel's hosting of it. (http://theaudacitytopodcast.com/chriss-dynamic-compressor-plugin-for-audacity/)

- **Levelator:** For podcasters who use software, this software is a separate free program that converts your sound, and balances it out. The software does require you to first export your file as a WAV file, place it in the program, and then import the converted file back into your audio editor so that you can export it as an MP3. You can find it here (http://www.conversationsnetwork.org/levelator).

Theme Music

Another element to consider as you produce your material is theme music. What kind of theme music are you going to use? Most of us can think of a theme that we would love to make into our own theme song. However, we forget about the issue of copyright. Because of the nature of music and the power of the RIAA, international law makes it difficult for others to use other artists' music unsolicited. So, your plans of opening your show with "The Final Countdown" are will have to be thrown out. But that doesn't mean you need to abandon the theme music. It just means looking to other sources.

Now, when choosing your music, it's worth considering the "Vibe" of your show. Is your show laid back, or energetic? Is it thoughtful, or comedic? Whatever you want your show to reflect, make sure that your music shows that as well.

One of the many sources for production-friendly music is the arena of royalty-free music. Royalty-free music is a special genre, designed for the user to make one single payment, and get full access to the music. This up-front payment method makes it fairly easy for producers and podcasters to find any one of many music publishing companies that produce royalty-free music. The one catch to these services is that the prices are fairly high, and may seem to be a big investment for a first-time podcasters. But once you've made the investment in audio, then you're the full owner to the track, and are able to use it to its fullest potential.

Another great source to look into is "podsafe music." The definition of podsafe music is

"a term created in the podcasting community to refer to any work which, through its licensing, specifically allows the

use of the work in podcasting, regardless of restrictions the same work might have in other realms."

This music was created by an artist, who stated up front that it could be used by programs like podcasts and online radio shows. All the user has to do is tell others that the creator made it. That way, they get credit, and attract more listeners. There are many independent bands out there that are focusing their energy on this musical method. What it does is allow others to introduce their content to others, and possibly attract downloads and live visits. It's a great way to introduce others to a musician's music, and serve the podcasting community.

So, where can you find royalty-free music and podsafe music? They are two different categories that are fairly easy to find.

There are a number of websites that I prefer, but the three best include:

- **Music Alley**: This website was designed by Podcasting guru Adam Curry, and holds a number of sources of podsafe music. This is a great source for music-based podcasts, or finding tunes for your website:

- **Royaltyfreemusic.com**: one of the top search sources, this website is a great source for finding music.

- **Magnatune**: This service provides a great source for finding albums and songs by undiscovered artists. What's great about their system is that they allow you to purchase over a thousand albums up front, just for 15 dollars. That is a lot of music, and is certainly enough to help you find that theme that you need.

- **Freesound/Findsounds.com:** Many people want to put sounds into their podcast episodes. These two websites are great places to look for sounds to reinforce themes, or transitions. What's great is that these sounds are free, and accessible. Make sure that you take advantage of these tools.

Exporting Your MP3 File

 Now that you've edited your podcast and it's ready to be released, you are going to have to export it as an MP3. Each piece of software has different methods for publishing your MP3. Audacity is the most complicated, because of the LAME MP3 encoder. Once you have this encoder, then the process is as simple as clicking 1, 2, 3. To export an MP3 file from Audacity, you just need to access main file tab on top. From there, you click "Export as MP3." This will send you to a page, where you'll redirect the save to your desired location. The computer will ask you to write ID3 tags for the file. After you click Okay, then the file will say yes, and it will be all finished.

Garage Band is similarly simple. You access the Share Tab at top, and then click "export Podcast to Disk." It will open up a window that lists both encoders, and file types. Choose "MP3 encoder" and "spoken podcast" for most shows, unless you use the Premium tools, and add photos to the file. Then, the file will be exported to your chosen folder. It's as simple as that.

ID3 Tags and Why They Matter:

You know how music tracks in iTunes show details like the artist, the album name, and even what year it was published in? This information is determined by a set of audio tags that audio engineers call ID3 tags. These tags are pieces of Metadata (Invisible information used for searches, and organization) that are editable by anyone. These tags include a number of details, including:

- Title (Example: "the 501st Paratrooper Podcast #2, The Band of Brothers in Easy Company"
- Artist (Example "Paratrooper Paul")
- Album Artist Name (this is the name of the artist, or collection of artists who made all of the content on the album)
- Album (Example: "The 501st Paratrooper Podcast")
- Grouping (this is a tool used in classical music. Nothing for podcasters to worry about)
- Composer (example: "Paul Smith")
- Year published (Example: "2011")
- Track Number (This is especially helpful with collections of songs or podcasts. It keeps things in sequential order.)
- Disc Number (of no importance to podcasters)
- BPM (not important)
- Comments (if a writer wants to write comments about track, they can. However, I cannot see many reasons to do so.)

All of these tracks are helpful in the organization. Podcasters should focus on the name, the artist, the album, the year published, and the track number. The track number is overlooked by too many podcasters, yet it is one of the most important ID3 tags, because that little number tag will keep your podcast in order when it is listed in iTunes.

Now, editing ID3 tags is really easy. You can edit them when you export the file. However, the easiest way to do it is to open the audio file in iTunes, and edit it there. That will give you the control necessary to create the best possible chance for someone to discover your show. Since search engines don't collect keywords and search terms from the audio itself, the tags are what are needed in order to be well-searched in iTunes. Also, they keep your podcast episode stream well-organized. This helps others to find the episodes they are looking for, and download it as quickly as possible.

Chapter 3: Setting Up Your Website

Choosing a Webhost, and Setting Up Wordpress

Now you have your content recorded, and it needs to be put somewhere. We could leave it on your computer, but then how would anyone find it? The important thing about podcasting is that you make your content available and accessible to as many people as is possible. What does that require? It requires a form of web presence. So, where should podcasters look in order to find the best possible hosting? There are a few things that podcasters should look for. The first is a high download rate. Since podcasts are mainly based on the download rates that listeners use, your website will receive a lot of activity. So, when looking at website bandwidth, keep in mind that if your site has a limit, and your show gets extremely popular, then there might be a problem. Podcasters often recommend looking at servers that have unlimited bandwidth. These website services do exist, and have excellent usages. Here are the two recommended services for podcasters:

- **Webhostinghub.com:** A web service that currently costs only 4.95 at a time, this service is perfect for podcasts. You only have to pay a close to 60 dollar payment once a year, and you get hosting with unlimited bandwidth, a free domain, unlimited email, and high quality customer service.

- **Liberated Syndication:** Another fairly popular service that is used by podcasters, Liberated Syndication gives you a unique package that is unbeatable. You get a set amount of "upload space." You can only add so many MB at a time for a month. The next month, it all resets, while archiving your files. These packages are very cheap, and

34

very profitable. LibSyn also provides a feed-tracking service, which lets you see the amount of downloads and visits. However, the website doesn't provide a great file host, since it uses the same template that is meant for the website. So, it would be recommended that you get a website somewhere else, and post a good portion of the files there.

Once you've chosen your service, you'll need to choose a service for syncing up your files, and posting them easily, and on a regular period. There are many tools that can be used by podcasters to complete this duty. The most notable is the weblog, or blog for short.

Most podcasts are hosted on blog-based websites that use a number of formats for content transfer. It is recommended that podcasters also use blogs. All blog-based content systems make it easier to post your episode, write a short summary, and send it across the web. The blog also instantly creates an RSS feed, which allows you, the content creator, to stream podcast updates to those tracking feed when they want to know.

There are a lot of blog programs out there for anyone to use. These include Tumblr, Myspace Blogs, Xanga, and many, many more. The two most popular blogging systems are Blogger (AKA Blogspot) and Wordpress. Both websites provide a basic blog that is customizable, and editable. However, Blogger is limited in its abilities to have creative themes, and to be hosted on another website. So, if you desire to post your content to a single website, then the best solution is Wordpress. Its open-source base has allowed for an infinite list of modifications, as well as a large community to rely on. This is why we are focusing exclusively on Wordpress in this blog. If you desire to explore other blogging software and how to podcast with them, it'll be worth searching online for other resources and tutorials.

So, how does Wordpress work? Wordpress, as an organization, allows the user two choices for hosting their blog. They can either post on their own individual website, or host their blog on their self-hosted servers. There are pros and cons to both of these options. By using Wordpress' servers, you get a blog for free. This free server does have limits, like a sub-par domain name (like myblog.wordpress.com) and the inability to post audio episodes without paying for an upgrade. However, if you host the blog on your website, you have almost unlimited freedom for edits and organization on the Wordpress blogging software. The Wordpress server used to require a little technical knowhow for completing the installation of the software online, but almost all web hosting services now offer a simple system for installing the Wordpress blogging system onto your website. If you do have to install it manually, make sure that you check out the Wordpress Codex for advice on how to do it.

Once you have installed Wordpress, it's time to start customizing your website. In order to use your Wordpress blog as a podcast-hosting website, there are a few things that need to be done. You will have to install a number of plug-ins, and choose a theme.

Wordpress offers a number of software bits called Plug-ins, that allow you to add features and functions to your Wordpress blog. The plug-ins spread out in purposes, and can do pretty much anything from allowing easy photoblogging, to posting your Twitter feed directly to your webpage to even creating a unique commenting service that resembles a social media network. Now, in order to use your Wordpress service for podcasting, it is recommended that you install a special plug-in that will allow you to just post your recording directly to your latest post, and create a file that is read by iTunes as a podcast episode. There are two specific podcasting plug-ins that are recommended by most podcasting experts:

- **Podpress:** This is the most used app for this podcasting. The plug-in creates a readable feed for iTunes, as well as a number of other features that allow for the users to create the most notable podcast episodes and feeds. While this plug-in is certainly good, it isn't the best choice. It has a few glitches and limits that make it hard. Nevertheless, this is a good plug-in for any podcaster.

- **Blubrry Powerpress:** After the creation of the Podpress plug-in, the podcasting company Blubrry felt like it needed to add its own software for its own users. So, they provided another great plug-in for podcasters to use called Blubrry Powerpress. Powerpress provides the best experience, as well as the easiest use. The service allows you to track downloads easier via Blubrry's website. This tracking is very important, and will be explored further later.

Both of these services are applicable for podcasters, and should be used to their fullest extent. These plug-ins contain a number of features, including being able to embed players within the podcast post itself, hosting advanced media files (like video and interactive files), tracking any episode plays or downloads, and even full support of content placed on iTunes.

What About Other Plug-ins? What plugins should a podcaster use to effectively use their website? There are quite a few of these programs that would be beneficial to podcasters and podcasters alike. This software will be able to help out any blogger or podcaster with a number of features, including the commenting, Tweeting, or even just adding pictures. Here's the list, from most important to least important:

- **Akismet:** This plug-in will delete all spam posts within a month. As you continue to create more content, this small piece of software will take care of a lot of your comments. It'll keep out the bad comments, and keep in the comments you want, so that you can continue to create conversation and community.

- **All In One SEO pack:** This plug-in will make your podcast more searchable. What it does is apply invisible tags (called meta-tags) to your website that will allow you to create a website that is as searchable as any other website. This is especially important for podcasters, since most of their content won't be very searchable.

- **Google Analytics:** Google analytics is one of the most helpful tools for tracking your downloads and website visits. What this plug-in does is add a small piece of Javascript to every one of your pages, so that you can track how many visitors you get a day. Very useful for podcasts that want to expand into monetization, or promotional work.

- **Sharebar:** This bar allows people to quickly post any one of your posts to social media, like Twitter or Facebook. By having this tool at the bottom of your page, people will be able to share your content with others a lot faster.

- **Contactform7:** This plug-in will create a contact form that will allow you to have others contact you quickly, without giving your email out via text (this open text makes it possible for spam bots to find your email, and use it to send you junk mail and scams).

- **Prettylink Lite:** This allows you to shorten links, which is important for any business. By shortening your links, you will be able to post the items quicker to social media like Facebook and Twitter.

Wordpress Themes

A Wordpress blog also requires a theme. Themes provide an appealing visual design for your website. These can be as simple as a white page, or designed to look like a control panel of a space ship. These design factors are easily chosen by anyone, though there are a few things to consider as you choose a theme:

- **Usability**: Does your theme allow for people to access your website easily? Everyone loves a great design, but if the design makes it hard to find the links to information, or even to load your page, then it may be worth considering changing the design to a much simpler format.

- **Uniqueness:** This kind of theme brings an altogether great design to your website. It leads people to look at your website and say, "Hey, I recognize this site, it's _____". There are thousands of Wordpress themes out there that will help you make your website represent your brand. So, make sure to choose one that allows you to express the vibe and persona of your podcast.

- **Customizable:** An easy way to create a web impression that is unique is using customizable themes. One great version of this is the theme that has a customizable header. By simply adding a simple header, you keep your website simple, while having that small flair that gives your website your persona. Often, you probably just have to put an elongated header with your logo on the side, or a few visuals that are reminiscent of your subject.

When Should You Start Publishing Episodes?

Most podcasters recommend after a few episodes. James Kennison of *Nobody's Listening* said that he always waits for 5 full episodes to be completed before he publishes his content. Why? Because if you have enough content, then you'll be able to provide a complete taste of your podcast, and your style.

People can listen to more than one episode, and figure out if they actually like it.

It also leaves a bigger impact on your web presence. If you jump into the iTunes directory with four or five episodes, you're more likely to attract websites and directories like iTunes. They'll publish your content in specialized areas, like New and Noteworthy, or Featured Podcasts. This is the kind of publicity that is perfect for new shows. It introduces your small name to a large audience, who are looking for new content.

Logos/Album Covers

When one wants to leave a visual impression, then they usually consider a logo. Logos provide a visual "brand" for your company. Think of it as a birthmark, or a specific facial trait that defines you. Without it, people wouldn't recognize you. For podcasters, this is   even more important. Their logo is also usually their album art. This album art is often the first thing that the listener engages with. So, by having a good podcast album cover, you provide a good first impression for your podcast.

So, it's recommended that you invest either time or money into your logo. If you are good with visual design, then create something that resembles the title of your blog, and makes people think of your topic. It also needs to be creative, and unique. The key to the logo design game is creating something that is memorable for you, and that makes people want to click on it in order to find out more about it.

Submitting Your Podcast to Directories

Your podcast is made, and you have a few episodes recorded and hosted on the website. Now what? Where are you going from there? The next step will be to get your show listed on a few directories. These directories act as a way for people to search out your content, and subscribe. The number one podcast directory is iTunes. There are tens of thousands of shows on this directory, and we need to get yours on there. The best tool for doing this is Feedburner.

Feedburner is a website owned by Google that manages RSS feeds for blogs and podcasts. The website is designed so that one can insert their blog or podcast feed into the website, create a unique feed for their website, and be able track the activity that occurs in connection to that feed. What's nice about tracing your feed through this is that if you change websites for some reason, you can simply change the feed location on your account, and the service continues to act normally.

Feedburner is used especially by podcasters. As well as tracking feed activity and stats, the website also allows you to add invisible metatags that allow iTunes to read you and your service. It also takes your RSS feed, and adds a few tags that make it readable by iTunes. These tags are especially helpful for getting placed in the correct locations in iTunes, so that you can get the most views and placed in the correct categories.

So, here's how to add your podcast's RSS feed into Feedburner, and then into iTunes:

- **Find Your RSS feed:** This feed will act as the key into any directory. For most Wordpress websites, you can find your RSS entries feed at mywebsite.com/feed/.

- **Insert Feed into Feedburner:** Anyone can place their RSS feed directly into the source. However, the best way to track the activity on your feed website is through Feedburner. This website will take your feed, allow for an easy optimization, and then make it so that iTunes sees it as a Podcast feed, with all of the necessary tags.

So just go to the front page of Feedburner, and insert your RSS feed's address into the slot, follow the steps requested accordingly and voila! It's in.

Feedburner.com.

- **Optimize Your Feed:** This will take a little work. First, access the Optimize Tab on the home page of Feedburner. From here, you just need to click on the

SmartCast button. You will then be sent to a page that has a list of categories and options that you need to fill in. These categories include:

- **Categories:** You need to choose the category that your show fits in. So, if your show is about photography, it would go under Arts < Photography. Some shows are harder to pinpoint. That's why you can choose more than one category.

- **Album Art location:** Make sure to have the direct link to your posted album art ready. That will allow for a quick Copy/Post to here.

- **Podcast Title:** This is the name of your show.

- **Podcast Summary:** This is where you need to describe your show.

- **Search Keywords:** These are the basis for how people will find your show if they use the search bar.

- **Email address:** This is used to update the owner if there are any problems, or contacts.

- **Explicit:** There are a few smaller tabs that are worth noting. The Explicit tab listed will state whether the show is Explicit (for adults), Clean (for all ages), or in between (content for older individuals). This term isn't terribly important, unless your show is based off of explicit content (such as crude humor, or sexuality).

- **Copyright:** If you or the company you work with desires to put copyrights on your product, this is the service that will allow you to do that.

Take Feedburner Feed and Place It Into iTunes

You now have an applicable feed for your company. It's time to take that feed, and insert into iTunes. Your feedburner Link should look something like this: feed.feedburner.com/myfeed. This website looks like this:

what your feedburner page will look like

This page is your RSS link. Now, you just need to copy the URL, and post it in iTunes. Here's how:

1. Enter into iTunes. Access the Podcasts Tab.

2. Look to the left of your screen. You'll see a link that says "Submit a Podcast." Click it. The page should look like this:

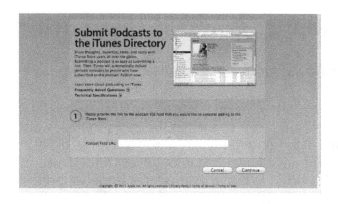

3. Once you're on this page, paste the link from your Feedburner website into the

   a. *iTunes Podcast Submission page*

   b. opening. You will see a confirmation page, and be sent back to the home page.

   c. You should get an update on when your podcast is on the directory within 48 hours. But that's it. Now, iTunes isn't the end-all. You will still need to continue to work in order to get people to find your show, and discover it.

Once the show is in the directory, it will be a lot easier for you to create fans, and attract listeners.

Your podcast is now finished. You've recorded a few episodes and released them to the world, and after all of this work, your show is now listed in iTunes. Are you all done with the work? By no means. For any podcast to be successful, it needs to be marketed to a larger audience. And that's what's going to be explained next.

Chapter 4: Podcast Promotions

How to Market Your Podcast

One of the most integral parts of creating an excellent podcast is being able to attract listeners to check out your podcast. Too many podcasters rely on a Field-Of-Dreams method of podcasting, which believes that "If you make it, they will come". While this model is hopeful, and will attract some listeners, the model is not one to live by. To create the largest possible audience, and have the largest influence, you will have to work for it. You are going to have to drop your name, and put links to your podcast in as many ways as is possible. There are a number of ways to do this. You can send out Podcast bumpers, use word-of-mouth marketing, offer up guest spots, pay for ads, do some writing for others, email many experts in your niche, use traditional media for press release placement and so much more. But before you get into any of this ,you should create a marketing plan.

Consider your podcast in the same way a CEO considers a business. Any business that wants to have an impact in the end knows that it needs to have a plan for advertising. Otherwise, it will not focus its energies in the right place, and will lose out in the end. Before you move forward with your show, you need to consider your plan for marketing.

So, when should you start marketing your show? With most podcasts, it's worth waiting to start your marketing until after your show has a few episodes. That way, people have enough content to whet their appetites. It also makes you look more professional.

There are some podcasts that can be enhanced by marketing ahead of time. Podiobooks (Books recorded as an audio book, then released as a podcast) do fairly well this way, since their release schedule is based on a limited release schedule. For them, there is a definite end, and a definite beginning. Other shows that are worth marketing ahead of time would be unique shows connected to time-sensitive activities, like season premieres, or special releases.

Whenever you start your marketing, it is worth considering what tools you have in your toolbox. The first step before launching your campaign is to research your audience. What shows do they listen to? Where should you focus your energies?   Build a list of shows where you might find a prospective audience. Start listening to them. See what they connect to. Collecting this information will help you make the correct contacts, so that you can use your time effectively, and leave the right impression on them.

The rest of this chapter will be dedicated to the multiple tools used for marketing. This will include visual ads, community marketing, promos, bumpers and much more. But to start if off, we will explore the world of Search Engine Optimization for podcasters.

Search Engines

 Most of us use search engines to find pretty much anything. We look for pictures, how-tos, news reports, even t-shirts. Search engines provide an easy and accessible tool for finding the information that we are looking for. Google is the number one search tool for most internet users. It uses a number of programs and algorithms to discover information and webpages? But how do you get your podcast discovered by Google and its competitors Yahoo and Microsoft Bing? All of these search engines catalog pages for different reasons. How do we optimize our webpages so that they are tagged and highly rated in as many search engines as possible? This is where the process of SEO (Search Engine Optimization) comes in. SEO is the process that websites use to make their website as searchable as possible, so that they get as high as possible on their respective search terms.

SEO is a tool used by many webmasters to make their content one of the top searches. And the tools that bloggers use will likely be the same tools that podcasters will use as well This toolbox contains a plethora of tools and concepts that will increase searches, including Metadata, backlinks (links directly to your website), information descriptions, and much, much more. SEO is often complicated, and difficult for most web users to understand. But in fact, it is worthwhile. We have to work harder in order to master it, but mastering it will allow you to attract the highest possible audience for your niche, as well as completing your project.

There are entire tomes written about mastering SEO and making your websites SEO friendly. Not that you need to read these books. Most bloggers and podcasters should attempt to get a basic understanding of the subject before moving forward, but they don't need to know everything about it. Blogging expert John Saddington (*Tentblogger*) once said that "one should create content for people, not robots." Saddington was specifically talking to bloggers who become obsessed with the process of SEO marketing. He believes that bloggers should learn and master SEO to the best of their ability, but they shouldn't worry about it to the point of letting it guide all their content. Instead, bloggers and podcasters should focus on creating excellent content and unique podcast episodes. After the content is made, they should then lace their podcast episodes and blogposts with the best possible SEO, so that it is easy to find, and easy to use.

Now, there are many parts of your SEO process for you to consider. The first thing to consider is; how SEO optimized is your website? Most websites are barely optimized up front. It take the webmasters a little work, and a number of plug-ins to create the best possible SEO content. Some basic tools you can use to affect your searchability are how you write titles, how you create podcast descriptions, and even the optimization of the images that you post alongside episodes. All of these adjustments involve the placement of unique keywords that you want mentioned in connection to your show.

Also, it's worth considering how to optimize your own website structure. By considering this, you will also affect how people explore your content, and how search engines will record your website structure. Things that you can do to fix this include changing the Heading, leaving "Breadcrumbs"(An organized link structure that is based on categories and sub-categories) for people to follow as they travel through your website, making your website load as quickly as is possible (most likely through a caching plug-in), and even changing how you post certain subjects, so that you will be tagged in a higher-ranking method.

All of these tips work for all websites, but what are things that podcasters need to focus on as they SEO optimize their website? When posting their episodes to the blog, they should create an attempt to create excellent titles and ID3 tags for their content. The more detailed the information is, the more likely it is that it will be tagged by a search engine.

Here's a good example for a tech podcast title: "Apple-tech cast Ep 41: Jobs leaves his job, 5 best apps for Twitter, and Solar-powered Mac?" This title contains all of the major subjects in your podcast episode. Then you would write in your podcast description a lot more information for you and your website:

"On this episode of the Apple-tech cast, Steve and Bill react to Steve Jobs stepping down from his position as CEO, Bill lists off the top 5 Twitter app that he uses, and Steve brings up a unique idea involved with Apple's next laptop." Then the description should also include a number of links to articles that are discussed, or tools mentioned. These links attract Search Engines like a magnet. Then, it's best to put your own website and email in it. This will allow you to linkback, and people are more likely to click the link as they are accessing the episode on their iPod. Also, don't be afraid to use the Tags tool in Wordpress, as well as the Categories. These are basic tools that will not only organize your website, but also allow you to put more tags out there.

Podcasters should also consider submitting their show to multiple podcast directories so that your backlinks will make you more searchable, and place you higher up in the ranks.

Another unique way to attract listeners is to transcribe your episodes. *The Quick and Dirty Tips Network* did an absolutely fantastic job of this. With each episode posted, they also posted the script that the host read from. What this did was make the content more searchable for websites, as well as make it easier for those who would rather read than listen. You would get more traffic from both audiences, and give them a choice of material. This method doesn't work with every kind of podcast. Conversational shows are particularly hard to transcribe. However, it can be done. The Mugglecast (*Mugglecast.com)* used to do that with their episodes. They hired volunteer transcribers to transfer their show into text. But most of us don't have their following, or volunteer base. So, if you do want your show transcribed, please consider the effort it will take before pushing forward with it. Maybe a far easier tool to use would be quick outline of what you talked about. Then you get the highlights of the show listed, which are what you want to use to attract the reader.

All of these tips are applicable to online websites. But this is only the beginning. You can find a list of links at the end of the book.

Marketing Via Other Podcasts

One of the great developments in podcasting is the inherent community that has developed around the show. Almost all podcasters have an understanding of the basic need for traffic. So, a lot of shows are happy to tell others about your show, as long as you tell your audience about them. This trade-off of marketing is really important for podcasters to utilize. It means that similar podcasts are not competing for an audience, but that they are sharing it. This change in perspective will allow for cooperation and a collective work towards bettering themselves, and creating a better product in the end.

Podcasters need to be using others for marketing. But how can you do that? The best form for this is the **Podcast Promo.** Promos are commercials made by podcasters that can be played by other shows. These promos are often a quick thirty to sixty second bit that is attempting to introduce themselves to another audience. These promos are your chance to sell you and yourself to another audience. But how do you leave the best possible impression?

- **Focus on your content:** Promos are a chance to simply introduce your product to the audience, not a chance to make an audio drama. So, think of how much time you have to express your information. The best format to use is 1) Introduce the show, and what's it about, 2) mention an example or two of notable episodes/conversations, and 3) make sure to tell them your website address and/or what to search for in iTunes in order to find your show.

- **Play a little bit of your theme in the back:** Your theme song is supposed to be part of your trademark. So, use that theme to leave an imprint on the listener. Just make sure that the music used is as low as possible, since you want them to focus on what you're saying. If you cover it up, then you will lose the audience in the end.

- **If possible, make promo relevant and unique:** In that 30 second window, you only have a short time to leave a good impression on the listen. It's worth attempting to do something unique, or creative. However, do not go crazy with this. You want to attract listeners, not scare them away.

After you've recorded this promo, it will be worth contacting a few other podcasters. Preferably, they are shows with similar themes to yours, and have an audience that shares the same interests. So, if you're a science fiction fancast, don't send your promo to a knitting show.

Email these hosts with a quick introduction of yourself, as well as an offer to play their promo. This kind of deal is a win-win situation for both sides. Of course, it is better if you focus your energy on shows with smaller audiences first. Most of the popular shows, like *This Week in Tech*, or *Extra Life Radio,* receive a lot of requests for promo plays. However, a smaller show will likely take you more because you are more likely to trade audiences.

Another creative way to introduce your show to a larger audience is through **podcast bumpers**. A podcast bumper is usually a short 10 to 15 second statement before a podcast starts. Here's an example of what I might say if I were to create a bumper for the Wired Homeschool podcast.

"Hello, this is Christopher Hutton, of Confessions of a Homeschool Graduate, and you're listening to The Wired Homeschool podcast, featuring John Wilkerson, AKA the Jesus Geek."

What I did there was introduce myself, name off my show, then lead the listener's impression back to their regularly scheduled episode. This is a simple marketing tool that introduces your name. It's especially helpful if the podcaster puts a link to your website in their show description.

What this tool also does is show your appreciation for the other podcaster. It starts a relationship that could progress into a mutual relationship, where you mention each other's shows often, and maybe even get a guest host.

Another great way to introduce listeners to your show is through **Inviting Guest Hosts.** Many podcasters will be happy to have a guest spot on your show. You can schedule them to come on, and either discuss a subject that they are an expert in, or interview them on the show. Usually, this requires both you to have Skype accounts, and for you to have a set-up that will allow you to record the conversation over the internet airwave. But what this does is attract new listeners to hear the interview/conversation with their favorite host. The guest will then advertise this specific episode through their social media because of their appearance on the show. People will click through, and you will gain visits, and potentially long-term listeners.

Traditional Ads

Even with all of the unique and creative forms of media, we often forget how well the simple graphic ad works. It's a tool that can attract viewers to your website.

Your most likely candidate for marketing use will be the simple Banner Ad. A rectangular panel containing the imagery of your show, the Banner ad is a great lead for any company. Now, these ads do usually cost money, unless you can convince a beloved fan to place the content on their website for no other reason than to support you.

So, consider banner ad placement to work like any other ad. You will need to confirm certain details in order to determine prices. Most blogs have an advertising rate card that determines what how much certain size ads will be, and how often they will show. So before you go further into this venture, it's time to consider certain factors, and how they will play into your ad placement:

- **Ad Size:** How big will your ad be? Do you want it as a header at the top of the website, or as a small side note?

- **Media Type:** A lot of ads are based on animated banners, which switch between images. So, do you want to use animated banners and ads? Or will you just have a single image? Remember, animated imagery is more likely to attract people, just as visually appealing designs do, but cost a lot more to produce.

- **CPC vs. CPM?** The two normal payment methods for ads are either Cost-per-Click (CPC) or Cost-per-thousand impressions (CPM). These two methods are completely different, and choosing the right one for your budget, and your desired goals is important. For example, the CPC model allows for an infinite amount of clicks, since you pay for the amount of clicks after the month. However, this can be expensive, and hurtful for the company. The CPM model limits your viewability, but that might be the best choice if your budget is limited. Both models are valid, but are best used in context of your product in general.

It's also worth considering audio ads. Some radio shows, and even some podcasts will make you pay for advertising. But it's just as good a model as attempting to get other shows to play your promo.

Some podcasters may want to consider an ad in a trade publication. This placement is great for people, and could introduce people who are less inclined to use new media to check out your podcast. So, if you are interested in an ad in a paper, don't be afraid of it. Check out the payrates and sizes that you want. It's also a good idea to hire a graphic designer to make your ad, so that it meets up with the magazine's normal visual specs.

But no matter what method you use for your ad, make sure that what you get out of the podcast ad will be more than worth the cost of the ad, even if that value isn't monetary.

Traditional Media

Yes, you may just be a regular user of new media, but that doesn't mean that you shouldn't consider using traditional media to market your show. In particular, podcasters should focus on using press releases to contact both their local and niche-specific news-sources. Any good podcaster should use every piece of marketing that he can in order to attract new listeners. So, what are some ways to involve traditional media in your marketing plan?

Press Releases: The press release is a great way to let local traditional media sources know about you and your new product. It's also a time-tested way of sharing time-sensitive updates, as well as attracting attention to a company. If you've seen, press releases are the way our government lets the media know about many updates. These updates are professional, trim, and easy to read. Podcasters who wish to have an impact should consider a Press Release for their show. But how does one write a press release? The press release should involve about three paragraphs that cover your point

- Write a title that is attention grabbing, and conclusive. A great example would be:

"Innovative New Media Producer Creates Imaginative Podcast about Sheep."

- Use your first paragraph to introduce yourself, or your company, and lead into your next paragraph, which will contain the heart of your story.

- This second and third paragraphs are the core of your material. This is where you are going to provide your concept. Your job with this part of the press release is to make your product look absolutely amazing and attractive. It also has to have a professional flair to it that makes it feel like the reader is a better person for reading it.

- The final paragraph is where you tell people where they can find your material, and how they can contact you.

This isn't a concise guide to writing a press release. It's recommended that you look into it further, and see what you can find out about the subject. There are numerous guides to this technique, so make sure to check out the list in the back.

Just writing the press release won't be enough. It's recommended that you do some cold-calling to the news sources you sent your press release, in order to get your press release into the news, even if it's a small bit in the side. In order to do this correctly, you should figure out which editor at the news source is in charge of your article's niche. The three categories to look into include Tech, Local News, and Style. Then, start calling these numbers. If you aren't able to get through, don't be afraid to receive a dial-tone. If you do, then just call back later. They will likely be busy with other stories. If they do answer, don't be afraid to discuss your story. Try not to take up all of their time. And if they reject you, don't worry about it. It's not personal. They just have a job to do, and your press release doesn't help.

Other Marketing Mediums

Flyers/Business Cards: When you go to talk to people, they may ask what you do. If you tell them that you podcast on the side, you can also give them a business card with more information. This gets them interested. It is a slower process, but it works. Also, fliers placed on community boards are another great way to attract traffic, and activities. This method is old fashioned, but effective.

- **Contests/Giveaways:** Many podcasts and blogs host contests in order to attract attention, as well as other followers. This will cost a little money, but people are always attracted to free products, and who knows? You may attract new listeners.

- **Free services:** By offering a free service on the side from your podcast, or making a business that is connected to your podcast, you could attract listeners and create a customer base for your products.

Conclusion: Podcast marketing has a number of tactics and methods. We've covered many of them here, including promos, bumpers, inviting guest hosts, normal advertising, press releases, and much more. But the great thing about marketing and advertising is that it is an open field. You can promote your show in whatever way you desire. In fact, creative and imaginative promotions are the best way to attract audience. When people see your commitment to that high quality promotion, then you will likely attract them.

My favorite was a method used by a frugality blogger to attract simple. She made a bunch of stickers that listed a domain she owned called "Igetfreebeer.com." This web domain sent curious Googlers to a specific article that she wrote about how she got paid to buy beer. It got her 300 new readers. While those 300 readers may seem like a small number compared to the millions that arrive at massively popular podcasts and blogs, it's still a valuable marketing strategy, because it's out of the box. As podcasters, we cannot forget that every person counts. And 300 is still 300 more people who read his website than before she sent out these stickers.

So, don't be afraid to take on a method that is both unique, and controversial. These methods are often worth the risk. They reach out to audiences that you may never have been able to access before. These kinds of investments are always worth it in the long run.

Because it could lead to the next big thing.

Chapter 5: Social Media for Podcasts

This is one of the biggest things you can do to market your show. Everyone is on some form of social media. So, one of the best ways to connect up with fans is allow them the chance to connect with the show in some format, or to "like" the show. This kind of representation is a good way to engage your audience. You have the opportunity to connect with you, talk about your subject, share links, and have some form of relationship. Also, it's a fantastic way to create something that will record the amount of fans, and allow you to keep them up to date with your material.

The top two social media sources that podcasters should consider using are Facebook and Twitter. Most of us know Twitter and Facebook. We use these mediums effectively every day, but what is the podcasting potential for these mediums? In what way can you engage your people through this? I hope to explore that question, and the answer for how to do it with both of these mediums in fuller detail. We'll start off by exploring the magical network of Facebook.

Facebook

Facebook is one of the largest social networks out there. With over 750 million users, it is a medium that needs to be used. Obviously, we all know how to create our own profile, and how to connect up with friends. But how can we create a page for our podcast? Podcasters should consider making a "Fan Page" for their podcast. A Fan Page is a page that allows people on Facebook to support you and your show. This page allows them to do this by Liking your page with a click, and start receiving updates about news from you. As more and more people click the like page, the number grows and grows, and as people see the updates you leave, they will also comment on posts and events as they occur. You then get the chance to talk to them back, and build the host/listener relationship. And that is very valuable. But how do you do this? Obviously, there isn't just a button up front that says "Make a fan page." So, how do you create this page?

- **Go to the Facebook Create a Page home (http://www.facebook.com/pages/create.php)**

Facebook creation page

- This page lists a number of categories for your podcast. Choose the category for your podcast. The best fit for a podcast would be to either set it up as either a Company, Organization, or Institution < Internet or Software or Website or blog < (Your category of choice).

- If you desire, you can sync this page up with your own Facebook account, which makes logging in fairly easy.

- Choose a photo. The best choice would be your organization's logo.

- You can import and invite contacts to like the podcast, or whatnot.

- Next, you'll need to list the website, and the details about the website.

- You have your Facebook page.

- It's best if you put out one or two updates for the users.

Now, you can post links to it via your blog, allow people to like it, and do so much more. But everyone has a Facebook page. How can you make yours unique? The best idea is to customize it and keep it up to date. Here are some tips for that.

- Create a Landing Page for those who arrive. These pages will leave a good impression, and introduce them to you and your brand.

- Constantly post links, podcast episodes, and posts that relate to your topic. Keep up your page, so that you don't have to worry about your content.

- Make sure to link to the page as much as possible. Every like counts, even if it comes from your next door neighbor.

- Don't be afraid to create content that is exclusively for your Facebook fans. Giveaways are always a great way to encourage loyalty.

Facebook pages are a great marketing tool for all businesses and websites to use. Podcasters need to emphasize it especially, since it involves social media and the internet. It's an opportunity to engage the world in as many ways as is possible. It's a window into Facebook, which is one of the largest social media windows for people to use.

Twitter

Any online marketer worth their salt uses Twitter for updates. So, your podcast should have its own feed as well. But how can a podcaster use Twitter well? First, you'll have to establish an account.

- Go to the Twitter front, and fill out the procedure.

- Choose a unique name that is either the name of your show, or a nickname for yourself. The show name is a far better choice, because it is a quick way for listeners to remember your name, instead of *Strudelcutie345*.

- Import followers from any other feeds. Since most people use the same email for everything, this import should bring a good portion of followers.

Now you have a Twitter Feed. What are you going to do with it? Each time you post a new episode, you should post it to your feed as soon as possible. It's that easy. But is that the only thing you need to do? By no means. With all of your social media, you need to engage your followers. This includes following others in your niche, finding experts to talk to, conversing with your people, and just being personable. But there is much more. Let's explore some good tips for Twittering podcasters to use.

- Post your episode multiple times on Twitter. This increases your amount of coverage for those who follow you, as well as increasing the amount of backlinks for your website.

- Use your Twitter background to introduce your show to others. It's a simple way to tell people about your show.

- Make sure to emphasis your brand, and your niche. Post links relating to it, reTweet those who are experts in your niche, and just focus on your niche.

- Respond to others, and add to their conversation.

- Just use your personal Twitter feed to market your show. That way, you seem more personable, and are more likely to interact with those who you need to engage.

This kind of persona is great for podcasters, who are trying to attract new listeners and followers. By being personable, constantly posting your material, and returning to your niche constantly, then people are far more likely to read your content.

Using Both Facebook and Twitter Effectively

Both of these two social networks are great tools for podcasters. But they need to be fully utilized. Jumping between both of these mediums is time consuming, and a bit obnoxious. So, what can you do? I recommend using an online website called Hootsuite. This website allows you to sync up many of your social media accounts, and post the exact same posts on all of them. This makes maintaining an official Twitter feed and Facebook page a lot easier. Just post the same content to both. Now, this does make it difficult for you to converse with the people. But this tool is still a great thing to consider as you push forward with the social media goals.

Using Other Mediums for Marketing: These two social networks are not the only two to limit yourself to. Try to find unique networks that will allow you to connect with fans in whatever way is possible. A number of networks to investigate include:

- **Linkedin:** This business-based social network may

be useful for helping others who are interested in your field find you, as well as other job-based applications. This is a good network to be involved in, but it isn't one particularly applicable for podcasters.

- **Myspace:** While this website is far less important than it was 3 years ago, it may be worth creating a page on there, and keeping it up to date for those still on that network.

- **Google+:** This is the social media network of the future. While people are still learning what they can about it, podcasters and bloggers should take advantage of it, and the liveblogging/podcasting it can bring. As of the writing of this book (September 2011) the network is not accepting new users. This makes it difficult to see what one can do with it.

- **Getglue:** This medium is still being explored by podcasters, but this company's potential make it somewhat useful for getting people to "Check-in" to the show, and show their support.

- **Social Bookmarking:** These websites like Stumbleupon, Digg, and Reddit can make it easy to share material to random individuals, as well as find material. So, use that resource as well.

Podcasters need to be active in these mediums. I order to create the best possible market, you need to work on learning and mastering the social media side of the story, and use if effectively. If you don't, then your influence will be drastically depleted, and unable to have the influence you desire. And without influence, your efforts will be ineffective.

Chapter 6: Monetizing Your Podcast

Like almost everything in life, Podcasts have a cost. Up front, you'll have to pay for web-hosting, a web domain, some recording equipment, and maybe even a web logo. All of these costs can add up. But what if you could cover the costs of the podcast itself? This is the suggestion that I offer. Podcasts run in a similar way to blogs. That means that they can be monetized in a similar way to a blog, relying on a mixture of ads, affiliate sales, and product placement. An intelligent use of these potential fund sources does take work and a little ingenuity, but it is doable.

Online monetization methods have a lot of variety. There are so many tools that companies use to market their material through outside websites, like advertising. They include advertising, direct sales and affiliate sales. Meanwhile, companies and individuals with podcasts can make money through merchandising, promoting a service, and even creating a Premium (AKA paid) podcast for those interested in donating.

All of these items have pros and cons that need to be weighed. But whatever your podcast is, it is likely that some form of income can be made from it.

Advertising

This is the most obvious method. By placing advertisements on either your website or in your podcast, you get paid a little money. This is applicable. There are a lot of podcasts that fill that role. But what companies are likely to market themselves with this campaign? Well, there are entire businesses that rely on podcast marketing to get shows. A pattern that we do see online is podcasters posting ads for a trial member ship with Audible.com, a popular Audiobook provider. I've found this ad in fan-casts, movie shows, book review programs, a historically unique program, and even a comedy show. Audible has spread its fingers out to the outer edges of the podcasting sphere This wide spread of advertising has gotten Audible many sales, and has attracted other companies to use podcasts as a marketing scheme. Web hosting service Godaddy and the web software developer Citrix (Creators of GoToMeeting, GoToMyPC) are two other websites that use podcast ad placement to increase sales and attract new users.

Now, it's also worth considering who you get to advertise. There are thousands of companies out there, each with their own ad style and product to promote. Make sure that you choose one that relates effectively to your brand, not just the first company you find. The more your brand connects with the ad, the more likely that you will get customers accessing it. Also, by connecting it to your brand, you are also saying that you approve of the product on its own merit. So, offering a review of the product on the podcast, or via an accompanying blogpost, will also increase sales. And as you increase the clicks on the ad, and the sales that the company gets, the more that company will invest in you.

Affiliate Sales

The internet has made the sales process a lot easier. And one of the most prominent marketing schemes currently available for users is Affiliate sales. How an affiliate sale works is simple: You place a link on your webpage. If a person click on the webpage and purchases something from the company, you get a portion of the funds.

This method is used by a number of podcasters. It's a simplistic form of advertising that allows the advertising company to pay you what your link is worth. This kind of business is one of the best. It's used by thousands of podcasters and bloggers. So, how can you find the best affiliates?

- **Find a Customizable Affiliate:** Websites like Amazon offer a strong source for affiliate sales. All one has to do is sign up for the Amazon Affiliates program. Then they can place links to anything in Amazon's market. And as people start to click on those links, their purchases of everything will give you an affiliate sale of up to 15% of the original purchase. This flexibility is extremely useful, for it allows you to sign up for one program, and offer sales for most products.

- **Go Specific to Your Niche:** There are affiliate sales programs for a number of unique companies. So, if your interest is in podcasting about stock trades, try and get one or two stock affiliate sales. That way, when people sign up, you get paid a bonus for them going through you. Don't be afraid to look further, and find listings of affiliate sales programs. Play around with them, and try to find out what works for you.

Affiliate sales is often one of the top three methods for making money online. So, investing your time into this model will be valuable, since it provides high quality tools for creating income.

Direct Sales

This method of podcasting is designed to sell and offer a product directly to the listener. This method is used by companies that provide a unique product, and want to directly introduce listeners to the product as a whole. This method is an effective way to get a product to a crowd. However, it involves a process that resembles the Home Shopping Network. While these might create great sales, it will decrease from your company's ability to create a community around your podcast, and maybe even detract from the content you want your show based around.

However, a company can easily do this. A great example of a model that uses this is Cliff Ravenscraft AKA The *Podcast Answer Man*. He hosts a show dedicated to helping people make their podcasts better. Along with that, he creates products for new podcasters that will help them to master their technology and methods. The material that Cliff provides on the show is inherently valuable, and great for all podcasters. However, Cliff does advertise these separate products, in order to gain sales, and support his family. And that's an admirable move. But the advertisements detract from the substance of the show, making it seem fleeting, and a marketing ploy.

So, companies can consider this technique for expressing their product. But be wary of the costs of directly selling your product to them.

Offering a Service

Podcasting is often a method used to market an entrepreneurial business, where a single person is an expert in writing/marketing/making money online/etc. This person offers his advice online via the show, but also has a service where they meet with people in-person/online to help them create a product/improve their craft. The host then mentions this task on their show multiple times. This method is similar to direct sales, and is a great way for a company to share their product/service with the world. However, the method sometimes hinders one's listening experience.

The marketing matters mainly on how the podcaster uses it. A subtle approach may attract more customers than a blatant approach. By focusing the show on the useful information instead of shameless self-promotion, the creator will look more professional, and attract more people. Also, their knowledge will be more appreciated, and they will gain a higher place in their community. Their expertise will be far more appreciated.

Merchandising

This method is used when a show becomes popular enough that people want to wear your logo in support. This is always a great step to take, since you'll be able

to see when people buy your product. While this isn't the best source for income, it certainly is an excellent tool to use. It's especially popular for fancasts that cover TV shows or film genres. The supporters of these shows generally enjoy wearing that kind of clothing, especially if it is witty. So, if you host a show about Macs, or the TV show Lost, you're more likely to get buyers of your shirts than the podcast about knitting.

There are a number of websites out there that allow you to print your logo on a product on demand. When someone buys the product, you get a portion of the funds, and an email saying that someone purchased your product. The catch for these products is that the podcasts are terribly expensive, usually ranging in the 20 to 30 dollar range, according to whatever percentage the creator receives profit from. Some of the best websites for this include Zazzle,

Cafepress, Spreadshirt, and Printfection. Zazzle is the recommended web-source because of its higher quality prints on shirts, as well as the ability to add your design to a number of products at the same time.

Premium Podcasting

This podcasting method was originally introduced by Paul Colligan, one of the original internet marketers to harness the power of podcasts. The idea of the service is that you (the podcaster) create a unique product that is valuable enough, that people want to pay extra money for it. This method is used by many full-time podcasters in order to make funds, and gain the support of the community. Cliff Ravenscraft is also famous for this. If you go to his website GSPN.tv, you will find a lot of unique content, as well as a link to his Plus Membership. What's unique about this subscription is that it doesn't get you just one show, but the archives to every show that Cliff has recorded since 2005. He also offers a number of other benefits, including a forum, discounts for events, and even the opportunity to be interviewed by Cliff himself on the unique *Community voice* podcast.

This kind of value has to be created over time. Not everyone is going to want to invest in this. But if you have a community developed, a large enough audience, and something valuable to say, then the service will sell itself.

Using Monetization Effectively

We all want to make money. And podcasting has a lot of opportunities to make money. The question then is; what's the balance? Too many podcasters make the mistake of emphasizing the financial gain of the podcast, instead of the community, or the content. This hurts the podcast's inherent value, and may even cause it to lose listeners. So, how can a podcaster balance out their monetization method with the need for good content?

- **Put the Audience's Needs First:** When choosing your monetization methods, consider what will be the most helpful for your audience. So, a life coaching podcast will certainly have benefits from advertising the host's other materials. Meanwhile, putting an ad for Audible in a knitting podcast may not be as helpful.

- **Should You Spread Out the Wealth, or Invest Deeply in One?** This is a classic method of investment technique. Investments 101: Spread the income out. This may mean putting a number of tools on your website that people may be interested in clicking. This method is a great way to create wealth, but can distract from the content. On the other side, you can invest your time into a single method of income, such as a tool that you swear by, or even offering your service to others. This allows your content to be more focused, but may lessen your potential income. So, consider these questions before you explore this medium further.

As you look into your media, it's always worth asking: is it time? If a podcast attempts to make too much money up front, they will lose a good bit of their authenticity. In the long-term, it will lose honesty over this conversation.

So, when should you start looking into buying advertising? Blogging expert John Saddington (*Tentblogger)* said that if you are able to get 250 unique visitors a day to your website (7,500 visitors a month), then you have a large enough number for blogs. While podcasters have a different set of

71

numbers, it's still worth waiting until you have a constant fan base.   By waiting until you're getting a constant download rate for each of your episodes, you will have a larger value, and will make more money in the long term from the sales and ads. Until then, keep producing content, attracting listeners, and marketing the show. It's all that you can do.

Chapter 7: Creating Your Community

Podcasting is one of those things that is extremely fun to do when you have a fanbase out there. People respect you, they send in feedback to what you say, and engage your material. They place banners, and they attract more and more listeners. They are total supporters of you and your enterprises. That sounds amazing, right? Well that is the power of community. It should be the goal of every podcaster.

Podcasting is the sharing of media. So, you don't do it just for yourself. You do it because you want to share something with the other people who like your subject. You want them to be anticipating your next episode. This support and excitement will lead to them engaging you, and engaging others in connection to your show.

But we should want it to be more than that. As podcasters, we want to engage the audience, to make them think, to make them feel, and to make them respond. That means that we have to get involved. And that is the pinnacle of all of the earlier work. We can get people to listen to our show all we want, but if they don't engage, then how can we know they're listening. Sure, we have numbers that say they are. But those are just numbers, not real people. We want real people to call in and leave their thoughts on what we said about something. We want the average person to email us about a question in your expertise, and then engage us over something that they disagree about. We want that social engagement, where someone says that they enjoyed what we put our heart into, or what. It's one of the core tenets of living.

And in creating that podcast, we want to add to other's living. Cliff Ravenscraft always has emphasized the podcasting community that he was involved in. He said that with every person he came in contact with who listened to his show, he tried to find out their name, where they lived, and one thing about them. This kind of investment is what has built his audience. It's what's allowed him to have the enormous influence he's had on podcasting in the last 3 years. It's what gotten people to invest in Ravenscraft's Plus Membership. He gave enough free content that they considered to be valuable, that he was paid for it in the end. Is that not amazing?

So, as you go forward with your podcast, consider this kind of community. You need to make it your final goal. It needs to be what you are looking for in the end. If you're in podcasting for just the marketing, or just the money, you're not going to get far. You're going to get something out of it, that's for sure. And whatever that thing is, it will be helpful, and good for you as an individual. But that doesn't make it the best thing to aim for.

How to Create That Community?

Community is a complex aspect of human life. There is no simple system that will forge the human relationships that are core to our communities. However, there are things that podcasters, who are the leaders in their community, can do to instigate growth, and encourage people to come back, to engage him and the others around him, and invest themselves in the podcast.

- **Emphasize Feedback:** Feedback is the way people contact you, the host if they have an opinion, or an idea that they want to share. If you want people to get involved, encourage feedback. Create a phone line that they can call, or leave an email address that they can contact you through. This method will cause you to dialog with others, and build relationships

- **Use Listener Contributions:** Don't be afraid of this content. Listeners often have unique things to introduce to you, especially since you aren't omniscient about your subject. If their content is mentioned on the show, make sure to give them the credit that they deserve. If listeners see that you care enough to use the content of listeners, it's a lot more likely to encourage listener loyalty. They will stick around, and be more likely to send you content for the show.

- **Actively Engage People:** When you get an email, make sure to reply as soon as is possible. That way, the people feel like they care. Same thing for Twitter. If a person reTweets your episode, or comments on your episode, make sure to acknowledge them.

- **As Your Audience Grows, Make Sure to Grow Abilities to Engage others:** Many of the more popular podcasters host forums on their website for engaging conversation, and creating unique material, and valuable concepts. These are great ways to get people to stick around.

- **Provide Content That is Inherently Valuable:** When people look for a product, they want it to be valuable. That's why many people support writers like Darren Rowse (Problogger) and Tee Morris (*Podcasting for Dummies*) These experts have provided high quality resources, and are constantly returned to as the expert. This kind of loyalty isn't easily manufactured. It took time, effort, and a lot of personal relations. And that's what you need to put into your podcast.

Remember: Community Takes Time

Community is a natural development that we cannot force. People don't like being forced into relationships. But that's what we try to do with advertising, with podcasting, and with being an expert. You need to let people make that kind of an idea. Let this naturally develop. As a podcaster, you need to make content that gets other to engage you and your expertise. You need to slowly put yourself out there, so that people can choose to engage you on their own time. So, don't think that you'll be able to create community and a successful podcast within a few months, or create content. It's going to take quite a few months, and maybe even years. But the investments that you make in people will have value in the long run.

Conclusion

Podcasting is a fine art, like any medium. That means that you can invest the highest amount of money, have the greatest looking logos, and sound like you should be on NPR. You can market your show to every corner of your niche. However, if your content is unhelpful and bland, you're not going to gain any traction. Podcasters need to focus first and foremost on creating content. Once the content is worth hearing, then it will also be worth investing in. Do your best to create the best audience, invest in them and their desires, and their goals.

Then, you can worry about things like making money and buying professional equipment. Even the best podcasts just started out with a couple of guys, a microphone, a computer, a website, and an idea. But that idea often blossomed into amazing shows, shows that made people laugh, that made people think, and sometimes, made people change.

That's the power of podcasting. It can connect with people, and make things happen. So, keep pushing forward with your podcasting goals. If you put in the work, the time, and just a bit of money, it will be worth your time in the end.

Appendix A: List of Links

Resources about Podcasting

Books

- *Podcasting for Dummies,* by Tee Morris and Evo Terra. This book is the basis for many podcasts. Morris and Terra provide intelligent and active tips for realistic podcast development. This book goes into the subjects covered here in great depth.
- *Problogger* by Darren Rowse and Chris Garrett. While this book is written for bloggers, it is still a great tool to consider using as you move forward with monetizing your podcasting endeavors.
- *Expert Podcast Practices for Dummies* by Tee Morris, Evo Terra, and Ryan Williams. This book is an extension of the first, and provides over 60 detailed explorations of the concepts required for the average podcaster. Another great investments

Podcasts

- <u>Podcasting for Dummies</u>: This companion series of podcast episodes for the original *Dummies books* provide a solid base to start on, though the content is out of date.
- <u>Podcast Answer Man</u>: This show is hosted by Cliff Ravenscraft. Updated weekly, this show is a great source for discovering new uses and applications for podcasting as a whole.
- <u>The Audacity to Podcast</u>: A unique show that focuses it's podcasting on the use of the Audio Editor

78

Audacity, as well as other features. Daniel is an expert, and is enjoyable to listen to for some great tips on podcasting that aren't covered here. You can also find Chris' Dynamic Compressor here.

Audio Editing Tutorials

- Audacity Tutorials: Official Tutorials, Audacity Wiki,
- Garageband Tutorials: Apple Garageband

Podcast Equipment Sources

Software

- Audacity: This free software is the perfect place for podcasters to start with.
- Garageband: This software is a higher quality than Audacity, and is free to all new Macs. However, upgrades costs 15 dollars on the Mac App Store.
- Adobe Auction: This software is used by professionals all over the place, and is a great place for professional production. The basic package costs 99.99, while the full edition costs a full 399.99.
- Apple Logic Studio: This is the fullest software for audio editors. While the cost is over 450, the program gives you great software, and a fantastic experience. There is a downgraded version called Logic Express that is more likely in your range of price.

Hardware

- Amazon**:** Great place to look for simple equipment, as well as software and potential music.
- Musician's friend**:** This store sells all variety of recording equipment. The best place to look for podcasting equipment is in the home recording section.
- Behringer Podcastudio: This studio is used by the author for his recording. Cheap set.
- Podcast Answer Man Equipment Sales: This website provides some of the best products for podcasters, and for studios that you want to take to the next step.

List of SEO guides

The Blogger's Essential Guide to Search Engine Optimization: John Saddington provides a high quality product for SEO newbies. Make sure to access his perspective on this subject for an in depth look at all sides of SEO.

-Google Webmaster Tools's SEO starter guide: This source is a great reference, since it comes straight from the ones you are optimizing for, Google. Make sure that you reference to the experts.

Appendix B: How to Do Basic Edits in Garageband and Audacity

Audacity

Installation: This may be a given, but it's the first step. The best place to get the Audacity Software is http://Audacity.sourceforge.net. As of the writing of this book, the most recent version will be Audacity version 1.3.13 (For Mac or PC)

Audacity Download Page

Just click on Download Link to the left. Download the most recent version, and follow the instructions. Once you have that, you will have the software fully installed. However, as a podcaster, you will want to release your files in an MP3 format. This requires a small piece of software called the LAME MP3 Encoding library. Without this small file, you will be unable to release your podcast in MP3. So, to get this file, just go to http://lame.buanzo.com.ar/.

A quick download of this file will be simple. Then, you just need to place the file in a location that is easily remembered, and accessible. Then, you just need to access Audacity. Start up the software like any other.

Now your software is installed. Let's get recording.

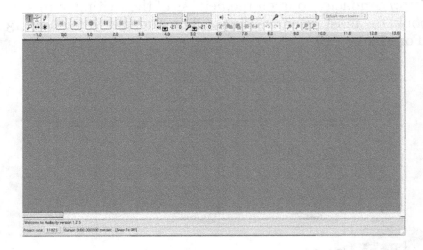

Audacity Main Page

The Basics of Audacity Editing

Here's a screen cap of the basic Audacity front Page:

There are multiple features for you to master. We will start with the basic bar to the left. The basic functions of this system are self-evident. The green arrow plays your audio, the red circle begins the recording process, and the square stops it. Check out the model below for further reference:

Audacity Page

Also, the buttons on the left are essential to the editing process. The I-shaped button is your basic tool, and allows you to select, delete, and control files as you see fit. The Envelope tool is the next tool, which allows for you to change the volume of the item over time. The pencil is your Drawing Tool, which gives you the ability to modify single samples. The magnifying glass is a zoom tool, which allows you to magnify one's view of a piece of audio. The arrow tool is called the Timeshift tool. It allows a user to take a piece of already-recorded audio, and move it along the recording's timeline.

Now that you have a basic understanding of all of the functions of Audacity, we can begin recording. Make sure all of your tech is fully hooked up, and that your primary mike is the one you want. (You can check this via the Preferences menu. You can find the preference bar either in the Main bar on a Mac, or access it in the Edit Tab). Then, click the record button, and talk away.

Now, after you've recorded all that's needed, you can go on, and start editing.

Here is a basic guide to removing sounds:

- Determine where the problem is. For the audio in the picture, I need to remove a small pause, so that the statement is more succinct.

Time to fix those unnecessary pauses

- Using the select tool, highlight the section that you wish to remove, like this:

Highlighting the audio as is necessary

- Now that the audio is selected, simply tap the backspace or delete button, and voila!! Your item is gone!

This kind of editing is simple. There are many other features that any podcaster worth their salt should explore in Audacity, but that is not the purpose of this book. If you want to explore the process of editing, check out either The Audacity Tutorials page or the Audacity Wiki. The number of tools for learning the software are numerous, especially because of the Open-source nature of this.

Garage Band

This software is Mac-centric, which makes it a bit of a nuisance to use for Windows users. Nevertheless, this software is great for podcasters and musicians alike. It allows for music creation, and for quick editing.

Installation: The great thing about this software is that it's already installed on most newer Macs. All you have to do is have the life software collection. This software is easy to access. However, if you do not have it on your Mac, you can purchase it from the Macintosh App Store for 14.99. Then you just download the file, drag and drop the application into your Application Folder, and activate it. Once you've accepted it as piece of software, then you can create whatever audio you need.

How to Edit and Record Audio on Garageband

- Once you've activated the program, you'll find a menu that gives you access to a number of features.

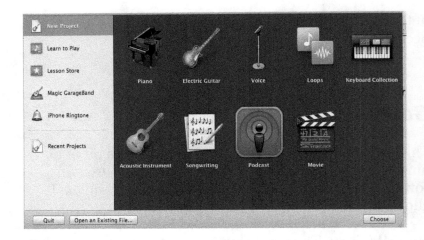

Main Page for Garageband

- Access the New projects Tab, and click on Podcast.

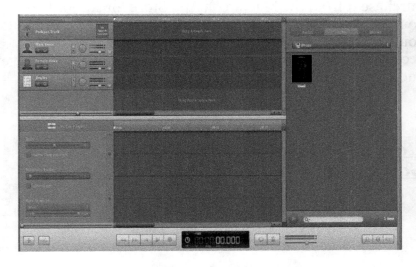

Garageband Recording Page

- The main window will open up, and the screen above will be visible. On the page, you'll see 4 specific tracks for recording: The Male voice, female vice, musical jingles, and Podcast track.

You will most likely record your audio in the Male/female voice track. These tracks are modified in a way that will allow them to enhance the human voice, and it's many sound modifications. Now, if these tracks don't work for you, you can add a default track, which will record the audio without any sound modifications.

- Hit Record. Your sound will appear in whatever row that you desire it to record in.
- Any editing that you need to perform will be in the lower window, which is a zoomed in view of the audio track.
- Use that lower window to edit, delete, cut, and copy audio. However, any audio that is cut does not immediately connect together. You will have to move it.

One of the nice features about Garage Band is the ability to make music using the loops provided. These loops can be combined to make a creative sound. The only downside is that every other mac user out there has the loops as well, and may have a soundtrack that sounds similar, if not the same.

Another unique feature is the ability to insert pictures into your podcast, as it plays. This allows the user to show images as the podcast progresses. This is great for certain shows, where visual examples are needed to help a person understand. My favorite example of this was *The Lost Podcast by Jay and Jack*. After the premiere of episodes of Lost, the hosts would post pictures of little things they noted in certain scenes. These were things that they felt were curious trivia, or integral clues to the *Lost* Mythos.

Now, this book doesn't even touch the full potential for Garage band's use. I recommend checking out any tutorials you can find on basic editing technique, or on how to use the many unique functions that exist on Garageband as a whole.

Also, accessing Apple support will give you access to many different kinds of tutorials for all their services.

Recommended Resources

- HowExpert.com – Quick 'How To' Guides on All Topics from A to Z by Everyday Experts.
- HowExpert.com/free – Free HowExpert Email Newsletter.
- HowExpert.com/books – HowExpert Books
- HowExpert.com/courses – HowExpert Courses
- HowExpert.com/clothing – HowExpert Clothing
- HowExpert.com/membership – HowExpert Membership Site
- HowExpert.com/affiliates – HowExpert Affiliate Program
- HowExpert.com/writers – Write About Your #1 Passion/Knowledge/Expertise & Become a HowExpert Author.
- HowExpert.com/resources – Additional HowExpert Recommended Resources
- YouTube.com/HowExpert – Subscribe to HowExpert YouTube.
- Instagram.com/HowExpert – Follow HowExpert on Instagram.
- Facebook.com/HowExpert – Follow HowExpert on Facebook.